Pets Are Awesome!

My
FISH

Norman D. Graubart

PowerKiDS
press.
New York

Published in 2014 by The Rosen Publishing Group, Inc.
29 East 21st Street, New York, NY 10010

First Edition

Book Design: Colleen Bialecki
Photo Research: Katie Stryker

Photo Credits: Cover weechia@ms11.url.com.tw/flickr/Getty Images; p. 5 Vlad61/Shutterstock.com; p. 7 iStockphoto/Thinkstock; p. 9 Vangert/Shutterstock.com; pp. 11, 17 bluehand/Shutterstock.com; p. 13 Beth Swanson/Shutterstock.com; p. 15 illuta goean/Shutterstock.com; p. 19 Arie v.d. Wolde/Shutterstock.com; p. 21 KidStock/Blend Images/Getty Images; p. 23 MattJones/Shutterstock.com.

Library of Congress Cataloging-in-Publication Data

Graubart, Norman D.
 My fish / by Norman D. Graubart. — First edition.
     pages cm. — (Pets are awesome!)
 Includes index.
 ISBN 978-1-4777-2866-6 (library) — ISBN 978-1-4777-2962-5 (pbk.) —
ISBN 978-1-4777-3037-9 (6-pack)
 1. Aquarium fishes—Juvenile literature. 2. Fishes—Juvenile literature. I. Title.
 SF457.25G73 2014
 639.34—dc23
                                    2013022429
Manufactured in the United States of America

CPSIA Compliance Information: Batch # W14PK3: For Further Information contact Rosen Publishing, New York, New York at 1-800-237-9932

CONTENTS

Fish are colorful pets.

A group of fish is called
a **school**.

7

All fish breathe underwater using their **gills**.

9

One of the most popular pet fish is the goldfish. Goldfish originally came from China.

All puffer fish have four teeth. They use their strong teeth to crush shellfish.

13

Epaulette sharks are some of the most common pet sharks. In the wild, they live only off the coast of Australia.

15

Bettas like to be alone in their tanks.

In the wild, the Boeseman's rainbowfish is found only in a single lake in Indonesia.

19

Feeding your fish can be fun.

If you take care of your fish tank, it will look beautiful.

WORDS TO KNOW

epaulette shark

gills

school

WEBSITES

Due to the changing nature of Internet links, PowerKids Press has developed an online list of websites related to the subject of this book. This site is updated regularly. Please use this link to access the list: www.powerkidslinks.com/paa/fish/

INDEX